I can't use you

until

I can free you

Georgia Barnes

I can't use you until I can free you

For Information Contact:
GLB Publishing
PO Box 388
Bristol, IN 46507-0388
ISBN 978-0-615-31512-6

Printed in the United States by Morris Publishing®
3212 East Highway 30
Kearney, NE 68847
1-800-650-7888

I would like to dedicate this book to my Lord God who has gently pushed me out of my comfort zone. I was content with these pages that I had typed sitting quietly in my computer, but God told me that He wanted me to publish this book and make it available for others to read. I want to be obedient to what He is calling me to do. My prayer is that this book would speak to the many women out there struggling with their self worth. And that it would help the men in their lives understand them.

For HIS Glory

Acknowledgements

First off I need to thank my Lord God for placing special people around me. Like when a baby girl starts to take her first steps, loved ones are there to encourage and cheer her on. That is the way it has been for me, so many people have walked along side me, encouraging me to carry out this mission. I would like to thank my family for showing me unconditional love as I struggled to walk through the darkness of my past to the other side. Especially to my wonderful, loving husband Bob, I truly believe God designed you for me. You always encourage me in the things that God has called me to do, thank you. To my dear friend Nancy Jenkins, thank you for editing the pages of this book with your expert eye to detail. And finally to my beautiful children, my gifts from God, I would not be the woman I am today if it weren't for you. I love you so much

Table of Contents

The more the words,

the less the meaning,

and how does that profit anyone?

Ecclesiastics 6:11

Introduction

How this project came about

It was 2001 when I started to feel an excitement in my spirit that God was going to use me. For the first few months I believed, watching around every corner to see if it was close at hand. I wasn't sure if it was a new job or if I was to move away, but either way, I knew God had plans for me. But as time passed, life started to push in on me, and I forgot to look for it.

I am a visual person. I saw myself walking down the road, my journey, my search. Along the way, I would stop to give someone directions. After I got them on their way, I would continue on my journey, but I was walking in another direction, forgetting about the original search I was on.

Several years later I find myself at another crossroads. With all that went on over the past year with my family, I felt I needed to journal all the questions running through my mind. I wanted to sort out my emotions so I could help my family, especially my daughter Ashley through hers.

I prayed daily that God would help my family know that He had their best interest in mind; that if they would put their faith and trust in Him, He would give them the desires of their hearts. I really wanted the kids to know that God created us all to do a job - a job that excites us, that makes our hearts jump, something we are passionate about. Especially now as Ashley and my son Kory both begin their adult lives, I prayed that God would direct their paths.

That is when I heard God say, "Do you put your trust in Me? If you want your family to know that I (God) want to give them their hearts' desires, you need to trust Me to do the same for you. Are you willing to put your trust in Me for your future? Are you walking with happiness and contentment in your life?" Again God asked me, "Do you trust Me with your hearts' desires?"

As I thought about what God was asking me and really got honest with myself, I felt something stir in my spirit. For years I have secretly had the desire to write and share how God has revealed Himself to me, and how He has answered my prayers, but I haven't had the confidence to put my thoughts on paper. The words of doubt echoed in my head, keeping me from pursuing it.

As I struggled with the thought of writing, I had all kinds of excuses. "What will people think? Will they judge me? Who do I think I am?" With each question I was reminded of a sermon I had heard. "If you are waiting to (feel) ready to do the thing that God is calling you to do, you will never do it. God wants you to lean on Him to do what He is calling you to do so that He can get the glory." I finally said ok, I will take a step of faith. I told God that if I was going to do this I needed a laptop in order to have the freedom and privacy I needed to write. The catch, however, was that I only had $250. "So Lord," I said, "if we are going to do this, You are going to have to find a really good deal."

With the help of a friend who understood what I needed in a notebook computer, I got on eBay and started to look. Several listings came up. As I watched the auction I realized my $250 wasn't going buy me the computer I required. I bid on a couple computers and lost just as I thought I would. I was going into this whole thing with a negative attitude and a feeling of failure before I even started. Again I could hear God say; *Put your trust in me, step out of the boat and get your notebook!*

Now, I don't claim to know how to strategy bid on eBay, but something told me to wait until there was about a minute- and-a- half left before the bidding ended. I kept myself busy while waiting, pushing negative thoughts out of my mind and repeating

9

in my head, *"faith as small as a mustard seed."* I also told myself that if this is what God is calling me to do then I don't need to worry about it. The time came and I placed a bid for $235.01, I was the highest bidder! But then I got a message saying someone out bid me and asked if I wanted to bid higher. I thought to myself, *"No, I guess that this isn't what God wanted."*

Something inside me pushed me, seriously, I felt pushed, and I placed a bid for $250.00. I won the computer, but with the shipping handling and insurance, the total ended up more than I was prepared to pay. In a way I felt I had failed. I went over the amount that I could spend. As I started to make the payment, I had a pleasant surprise. Bob, my husband, had sold some tools on eBay and we had money in our Pay Pal account. So, the total was not much over the initial limit I had set. This confirmed what God was saying to me. Setting aside worry, I put my faith in God and He saw me through. *"Now what God, what is it You want me to say?"* Here I go stepping out of the boat...

Delight yourself in the Lord and He will give you the desires of your heart. Psalms 37:4

Chapter One

The Call

I was in Chicago at a seminar for work; it was to run Friday evening, and all day Saturday. As my co-workers and I entered the auditorium Saturday morning, we automatically checked to make sure that our cell phone ringers were off. With a room full of people, no one wants the embarrassment of having their phone ring while a speaker is on the platform talking.

The room began to fill quickly with chiropractors and assistants from across the country, expectant to learn and glean new knowledge from the seminar. I could feel the excitement start to build. As I listened to the presentations, I started to relax a little and really take note of the information that was being shared. Before I knew it the morning had flown by and it was time for lunch.

I really didn't want to be there. At other seminars I had attended I would get overwhelmed with the new information (sometimes too much information).

It was a beautiful June day. The excitement that I felt inside the conference room seemed to flow out into the streets. The busyness of the city had a sparkle about it - the sun dancing off the building windows, cars passing by, and people walking on the sidewalks. Even the streets were lined beautifully with flowers. It really felt good to be outside. A group of us walked a few blocks away to a restaurant for lunch. I felt pumped up about my job and thought maybe this _is_ the career that I was going to settle into.

As I was listening to the talk around the table, I realized I had forgotten to turn my phone ringer back on. As I looked at my phone I saw that I had four missed calls. Scrolling down the list of numbers I started to feel anxious.

At the time, I didn't realize my boss had excused himself from the table to get a call on his cell phone. Coming back to the table, he walked directly up to me, and quietly told me that I needed to call my husband Bob right away.

Oh my God! I instantly felt my heart in my throat and asked nervously, "_Why?_" I was directed again, with all seriousness to call Bob. So, I excused myself from the table and made my way to the ladies room, to call him. Almost too afraid to move, I dialed the phone.

My friend/co-worker came to my side just as Bob picked up. I don't know if she knew anything or not, but I was thankful that she was there. Bob's words didn't seem to connect in my brain. It was like I was in a dream. I could not understand. How could this be?

Bob told me, in a steady voice, you must leave the conference. Ashley is in the hospital in Kentucky and needs you right now. *Oh my God!* I asked what happened, but Bob wouldn't tell me. *I have never been so scared in my life. My baby was in the <u>hospital</u>, she needed me, and I was so far away.*

It would have taken too long for me to drive back home to Elkhart and then down to Louisville with Bob, so I got a flight to Kentucky from Chicago. My co-workers and boss's wife helped me with the flight details, gathered up my things and put me in a cab to the airport. I have never, had terror wash over me that strongly. It was paralyzing. I could not think, make decisions or even form words to describe what I was thinking or even feeling.

The "*what ifs*" were scaring me to death. I knew I had to pull myself together; I had to push fear out of my head like never before!! "What could be wrong," I thought to myself. Ashley can't be going through another crisis so soon. Just two weeks prior Ashley had lost a very dear friend in a fatal car accident.

The phone call 2 weeks before

I missed the call from Ashley the night that she got the news about her friend (*we will call him Braden*). When I heard her voice on my voicemail my heart was instantly heavy. I couldn't understand everything she was saying, but in my spirit I could sense her pain.

I called Ashley back as soon as I got her message. Between sobs she told me that after attending the prom with Braden he was in a fatal car accident on his way home from dropping her off. I wanted to hug her so badly and be there for her. *All I ever wanted was to keep as much pain away from my children as I could, but I can't, and it just rips my heart out of my chest.*

Once we got the details about the funeral, Bob and I made arrangements for Ashley to fly home. It would be two long days before we could see Ashley face to face and be able to hug her and let her know that we were there for her. I couldn't imagine the pain she must have felt. Ashley talked to Braden often, sharing any and everything that was on her heart. They were very close.

When Ashley arrived though, she didn't look as emotionally devastated as I had anticipated after hearing her on the phone. In fact, as she walked up to me she smiled and talked about her flight. She looked emotionally stable. It was almost scary how calm she was. She had two days to prepare herself, to turn off all those emotions and feel nothing.

How much suffering has my little girl gone through before now to be able to stuff something so painful, to become so numb to her own emotions?

Bob and I went to the funeral to give Ashley emotional support, but I was the one who had a hard time keeping myself together. Braden was such a wonderful person, and so young. I couldn't even imagine what his parents were going through. On the way to the funeral I prayed that Braden's family wouldn't treat my little girl badly, and that they would understand that she was hurting too. I was so proud of Ashley at the funeral. She was so poised and compassionate. At the very end of the funeral, Braden's mother called out for Ashley. Once she made her way through the crowd of mourners, Braden's mother grabbed Ashley and hugged her and told her that they did not blame her for Braden's death, and that she shouldn't blame herself either. She went on to tell Ashley how much Braden enjoyed their friendship and how much joy she had given him by being his prom date his senior year. I can't tell you how much I appreciated Braden's mother for showing my little girl compassion and love. God had answered my prayers.

We were invited to attend the dinner that followed the funeral. I watched Ashley as each family member gathered around her, asking her questions about their night at Braden's prom. I could see genuine joy on her face as she shared the details of the night. Braden's family was touching Ashley's arm and hugging her, totally captivated as she described the night. I believe she gave them a gift, a glimpse of their young man treating Ashley as a queen, yet, being his fun-loving self as he took her to his special event. As she spoke there were smiles on the faces of everyone who was listening, as if they were right there enjoying the moment with Ashley and Braden.

I thought to myself she is being strong. Look at her. I know this is tearing her up inside, but she is being strong for them.

I could tell that she was exhausted, keeping it together. On the way to our car to go home Bob put his arm around her. Only then did she allow herself to feel the impact of the day, and she collapsed into her dad's arms. She cried herself to sleep as we drove home. I prayed that God would ease her pain and wrap His love around her. *I believe with all my heart that Braden is with our Heavenly Father.*

16

Waiting for my flight to Louisville

I was still in shock when the cab driver dropped me off at the airport. It was quite obvious I was a total wreck. Thank God there were people to assist me to the right gate. At the airport I had to focus on other things - on God's promises and on any scripture that I could remember. I read Psalm 23 at my grandmother's funeral, and all I could say over and over in my head was, "Even though I walk through the valley of death, I will fear no evil, for you are with me." "You are with Ashley!" Repeating the last statement over and over "You are with me. You are with Ashley." I kept telling myself that God was with Ashley. She was okay. God will help us get through this. Then in my spirit I heard, "We go through things so that we can help others go through similar things." With that thought, I knew deep down inside that Ashley had been assaulted. I didn't know the details, I didn't even know for sure that she had been assaulted, but to keep fear out of my heart and not guess what had happened, I had to stand on my faith that God is good and He was with her.

The time wasn't moving fast enough. I was gripped with fear every time the enemy told me a lie. It was a paralyzing fear, a fear that I hadn't felt before for my children.

Oh, the enemy is manipulative! He knew just what to whisper in my ear. Things like, "How can you be so sure Ashley is okay? How do you know it was an assault? Maybe it was a bad car accident like Braden's? Maybe she is hanging on to life right this minute. How can you be so sure that God is with her? If He was with her in the first place she wouldn't be in the hospital right now."

With every attack, I fought back with the image of my daughter in my Lord's hands and HIS heavenly glow all around keeping the darkness out of her hospital room. I prayed His covering over Ashley and kept focusing on that picture in my mind.

I not only prayed for Ashley but for Bob as well. He had told me that he didn't think he could handle it if anything happened to any of us; Ashley, Kory or me. I also knew how reckless a driver he can be when he is upset. I never thought he would be in Kentucky shortly after I landed.

When my sister- in- law Randi picked me up at the airport in Kentucky, she gently told me that Ashley was found in an alley and that the authorities believed she had been drugged and assaulted. Those words tore my heart. I could not let my mind visualize what she had told me. Again I had to visualize God with Ashley as we headed for the hospital. Weaving in and out of traffic, I felt that I was in a totally different world. All the sudden, Louisville wasn't the beautiful town I once believed it to be. Now it seemed ugly. It was like I had a different pair of glasses on and I felt the darkness in my spirit. As we got closer to the hospital I was overwhelmed with all kinds of emotions. I knew I had to pull myself together. I didn't want to cry in front of Ashley, or Bob for that matter.

When Ashley and Kory were younger, they would get very upset when they saw me cry. It didn't matter if my tears were from joy or hurt. When I cried, they would start to cry.

Not really sure how to act, I was somewhat timid walking into the hospital room to see her. I didn't want her to think that I was judging her, or that I was disappointed. What I wanted was to tell her how thankful I was that she was alive, to give her a hug, and to paint her world full of beautiful color, to stand between her and the darkness that she was now experiencing.

I asked God, how could I show her that I love her so much it hurts? She doesn't like it when I baby her. But is this time okay? How much emotion can I reveal to her?

When I walked into the room, Ashley almost looked disgusted that I was there. She told me that she didn't want me in the room and to wait out in the hall.

I could understand that, but the look on her face when I entered the room told me what I already knew. She didn't want me to baby her. She was going to be tough for everyone and harden herself so she wouldn't feel anything.

After the hospital

By the time the formalities and all the precautionary steps were taken, it was after midnight when Ashley was released. She was there for over 12 hours. Ashley was exhausted and didn't want to deal with her dad, Aunt Randi, and definitely not me. Her friend, Katie, who had been with her at the hospital, drove us to Randi's house. She tried to make small talk with Ashley and me, but to tell the truth I was too busy trying to size up Katie. *Good influence or bad?* It seemed she genuinely cared for Ashley's well being. I was thankful for that. Katie was like a big sister to Ashley.

We pulled into Randi's drive and Bob met us at the car. He was dealing with this whole thing as any father would - wanting to cuddle his little girl, but not wanting her to see his tears. Bob was absolutely devastated. The emotional roller coaster that Bob was on was heart wrenching. He had extreme hate and anger, and indescribable hurt. Hurt that is so deep that your heart and soul ache. *Lord a part of me wants to crawl in a cave and shut down, but I can't, I won't! Help me be strong for my family.*

After Ashley showered and ate, I tucked her into bed and prayed over her - something that I had missed doing with her for what seemed like years.

I could understand some of the emotions that Ashley felt, but I didn't know how to identify with Bob. He has always had a warrior spirit! Bob may have been busy working most of the time the kids where growing up, but everyone knew not to mess with Bob's family. It is his natural instinct, it is who he is, a defender. As I tried to get Bob to calm down and convince him not to take vengeance for his own, at least for that night, we just cried.

I kept asking God to help me be strong, and to help me stand on my faith. I felt like I was in a small boat in the middle of the ocean taking on water. I was franticly trying to throw a life line to Ashley struggling in the angry waters on one side of the boat while Bob was struggling on the other side.

We have been through different types of hardships before and God has seen us through. This time was going to be harder, and we agreed that we would need to get help processing all that had happened, to understand that this tragedy had affected each of us in a different ways. We needed to learn how to respect each other's emotions and to patiently allow each other to process this in our own ways.

Dealing with or stuffing emotions

Once we got Ashley home to Indiana, Bob and I thought a job would be good for her. She could save some money living at home, and she could talk more easily about the emotions that she was feeling.

Bob's place of employment was hiring a line worker, so Ashley filled out an application and began working three days after moving home. But as each day passed, I wasn't able to talk to her. She left for work early, before me, and got home early, again before me. I was working almost 12 hours a day and by the time I got home she was already gone. I wasn't sure how she was doing emotionally. Every time I got a moment with her I felt I needed to dive right in asking her questions, but that only pushed her farther away from me. She showed no emotion whenever she talked about the things that had happened over the past several months. She detached herself from it all and stuffed all those emotions. They were too hard to deal with. I know from personal experience that stuffing your emotions leads to numbness, anger, bitterness and even hate. Keeping herself busy, she didn't have to think about all that had happened. I don't blame Ashley; sometimes it is easier that way.

I remember detaching myself from hurtful things in my past. It hurts too much to <u>feel</u>. It is a lot easier just to cut that part out of your heart and move on with life. *I asked God, "How did I process emotions from my past?"* I want to help Ashley process her feelings, not so that she can hurt, but so that she can live and know the truth of what You, God, say about her.

Chapter Two

Stirring up deep emotions

I was watching "Cold Case" on television one evening about a month before Ashley's assault. This particular episode was about a young girl whose parents made her go to a Catholic school for unwed pregnant girls. It really struck a cord with me, and I started to cry. I could identify with the story, but it was a memory that I had stuffed so deep in my soul that I had convinced myself that it wasn't real. I hadn't really thought about the months that unfolded that one summer of my life. In fact, it was a time in my life that I thought was closed, dealt with, and put away. Never to be remembered again.

When I was 15 years old - I was also taken advantage of, looking back now I realize how very naïve I was. The assault resulted in a pregnancy. I was so young and too scared to tell anyone what had happened to me until I was several months along. To this day I don't really remember how I told my parents. But not long after they found out, I was sent to a school for young pregnant girls. The TV show's story line was similar to my life, a part that I had forgotten. Just like the girl in the story I felt like an outsider. I felt like I didn't belong at that school, that there was something different about the other girls. As I continued my normal studies on my own the other girls were learning how to care for their babies once they were born. And just like the television show, adults would lower their voices to a whisper when I was around them, usually at the doctor's office or when I went to the store with my mom.

Then it dawned on me that maybe I hadn't really dealt with all those emotions. That maybe I had blocked out more than I realized. *Was I still in denial?* How could I help Ashley deal with her emotions and pull her out of her denial if I hadn't dealt with my own past, my own emotions? Then all of the sudden, feelings of shame, guilt, and failure overwhelmed me as my mind went back to when I was in high school. I thought that all those feelings and emotions were gone, that I had dealt with it. *Lord, how did I deal with my past?* I didn't.

I turned myself off…

During the pregnancy I disconnected with reality, "*This* wasn't really happening to me." I remember telling myself, "This is just a dream, a bad dream," as my body went through the changes. I don't remember playing with dolls a lot when I was younger, you know pretending. But that is what I did; I was pretending that the changes that I was going through were happening to someone else, not me.

I cared for a pet...

It is interesting to me how God's littlest creatures can comfort us, be there for us. I'm talking about a baby bunny that I called Phyllis. I had a lot of isolated days. Not only did I no longer going to school with my friends, but I pulled myself away from my family too. My time was spent with Phyllis, taking care of her and playing chase out in the yard. It was like she was my puppy. Phyllis was kept in the house when she was very little, but when she got bigger, she was kept in the garage. One early morning I went out to visit her, but she was gone. I was looking for her and calling out her name, but that was the morning I went into labor so I had to end my search, never to see her again.

I have wondered about Phyllis many times throughout the years, and I asked myself, "Did God give her to me to help me?" Was it a coincidence that she was there the whole summer to keep me company, and then was gone the very morning I went into labor?

Years later…

After graduating from high school I kept busy going to parties. It was easier pretending to be someone else once I got out of school. I could be anyone I chose to be. I rarely gave out my real name to the new people I met. I felt that if I share my name, people would automatically judge me. That once I said the name "Georgia" all my shame would be exposed. No, I didn't like Georgia. At times I hated her. I was more comfortable just erasing that person out of my memory.

When I got married I was busy being what I <u>thought</u> was a perfect wife and mommy. I put extreme pressure on myself to get things right or perfect. The house had to be very neat and tidy. I was so bad that if the kids walked away from their toys to go to the bathroom, I had everything cleaned up and put away by the time they came back. I was told that my house smelled like a public pool because of all the bleach I used to clean. Yes, staying busy kept my mind from thinking about all the ugly things I felt about myself.

It had been years since all of that happened. I really thought I had dealt with it already. Why were all these emotions flooding back?

Chapter Three

Lord what are You calling me to do?

I was struggling, trying to understand what God was calling me to do. I wanted to help Ashley understand that the things that had happened to her didn't make her a bad person. I wanted to spare her from the trap of negative self talk and low self esteem that I had endured. It is an awful trap that I have to be careful not to fall into to this day.

I have always said to my children that things don't just happen. There is a reason for everything. There are no coincidences with God. Our lives are God appointed. But how was I to explain that to Ashley? I didn't even understand why it all had happened to her. How could I answer her questions why? God, why?

Then I started asking myself honestly if I had examined the scars that were left on my heart. *"Surely I have, Lord," I thought. "I am okay, no real emotional problems here. God, you are not asking me to dig deeper, are you?"* I just wanted to help Ashley, and so I asked God, "What is it that you want me to do? This isn't about me, Lord; this is about Ashley...healing for her. I am okay."

Leaving my job to pray

Having worked in a chiropractic office for several years, I was flattered when I was asked to help start a new office, flattered, but on the other hand, afraid of failing. *How could someone put so much faith in me?* The office had opened in April, and even though the doctor had clients from his old office, it was still a new office. There were documents to make, a new computer system to learn, procedures to implement, and insurance guidelines to know. I prayed every day for wisdom. I wanted to make sure everything was right for the doctor, but I was being spread too thin.

The first few months, I thought I would lose it. My job was the only thing I thought about day in and day out. I lost sleep, and it was the topic of my conversations with Bob. He hated the fact that the office was draining me mentally and emotionally.

Once I got back from Kentucky, I went back to work. It was total craziness for me. Dealing with my raw emotions from Ashley's assault and from my own past, on top of my new responsibilities, I knew in my heart I couldn't do it. One afternoon, everyone in the office was gone for lunch except for the doctor and me. Doc asked me, "What can I do to help? What would make it easier for Georgia?" *I think he knew that I was struggling. I believe he wanted what was best for me and my family.* I didn't know how to answer him. I didn't want to disappoint him. That's when I felt a push from God. Seriously, I had no intentions to say what I said. "I think you need to find a replacement for Georgia." *As soon as I said those words, I felt like throwing my hands over my mouth. What did I just say?* Doc then proceeded to ask, "Replacement for the clinical part or the billing part?" Again, I felt that push and said, "All of it!" He asked, "Are you saying you want me to replace you?"

"Yes," I said.

For the next several weeks Doc searched for a replacement. When we had time to talk, he asked me about Ashley. He asked questions like, "What is it that you think you can do for her?" *He meant once I was home.* "Doc, you may not understand," I answered, "but if the only thing I do at this point is to intercede for my family, than that is what I will do, because there is power in prayer."

Eight weeks after that conversation I resigned, and was home, making myself available for Ashley whenever she wanted to talk.

Now what?

I kept asking myself over and over, "What can I do to help Ashley?" Everyday I prayed, "Lord, help me help Ashley. I know what she is going through." I wanted to fix it for Ashley, to take the hurt and pain away. Even though she didn't cry, I knew she was hurting. "How do I start to fix it, Lord? How do I help her?"

I didn't want to make her cry or feel bad things. I found myself walking on egg shells. I wanted her to know that I was cheering her on and wanting her to push through this horrible thing that had happened to her. I wanted to tell her that she that she was very precious to God and to all of us, to assure Ashley that God loved her and that He would never leave her. But from Ashley's perspective, God did leave her. In her mind, God allowed those things to happen to her, and she could not trust Him.

Again, I asked "Lord, how do I help Ashley deal with this, to identify with her emotions and let the healing begin?"

Bob was trying to deal with the fact that Ashley's attackers had gone unpunished. He couldn't understand why she didn't want to go after them. I tried to explain to him that the scariest part for her was that she was drugged and didn't remember everything that happened.

Because of my experience, I knew the thoughts that most likely were going through Ashley's head questioning if it was her fault and wondering if she had done something she would be ashamed of.

I tried to tell Bob to picture himself on one side of a swamp (the past), and me on the other side (the future) with Ashley in the middle, stuck in the muck. Bob wanted her to recall that night to go after her attackers, and I just wanted her to move past it. And Ashley was stuck in the middle, in the muck, not moving at all. Ashley needed to know that we loved her and that nothing would ever change that. She needed to see herself as God sees her, not as the enemy wanted her to see herself, which was a lie.

I know about those lies, I lived with them for years not knowing that I had a purpose designed by God himself. I saw myself as someone who was disposable, dirty, and a failure; always trying to get approval. These feelings came, not only when I was young, but also as an adult. Once I got married, those negative thoughts became louder, and louder, making it hard for me to keep my feet grounded in reality. I felt I was failing as a wife, mother, daughter, and sister. And as I believed those lies, my soul was being destroyed. I did not want Ashley to battle the same negative self talk that I once experienced, or the loneliness I felt. It took me many years of reprogramming those negative thoughts.

I would pray to God and ask Him, *"How do I reach her? How do I get Ashley to open up, Lord?"*

The Flowers

After a few weeks, I still had not connected with Ashley. I decided that God was, in fact, calling me to intercede for my family. I was okay with that because there is power in prayer! It felt good to know what I was called to, and I felt a load lifted off my shoulders. I thought, *Phew! I did not have to deal with the past.* Later that day, I found myself at Menards, even though I really had no reason to be there. So I decided to go look at the flowers. The mums looked so beautiful, I decided to buy some. I picked out the colors I liked, and placed them in my cart. I then noticed the tags of the other flowers on display, "That's strange," I said to myself, "these flowers have real names." As I looked down and read the name of the mums that I had picked my heart started pounding faster. Tabitha. *Tabitha was the name my mother had put on the original birth certificate of the baby girl I had when I was 16.* I tried to brush it off, but when I went to go pay for my flowers, the cashier pointed out to me that the mums had *real* names, not once, but three times. The conversation went like this:

"What pretty flowers you picked out today. Did you notice that they have real names?" the cashier asked.

"Yes I did," I responded back.

"Yeah, and did you see that big beautiful mum sitting in front of the display? Isn't that beautiful? And the flowers have real names."

"Yes! That is a beautiful plant," I said.

"The names are beautiful, too, those are real names, you know," she again said.

It started to freak me out, and I got really nervous. I paid for the flowers and hurried to my car and once I got there, I had to just sit there for a moment. My heart was pounding hard and my head was spinning as I thought about what had happened.

"Yes, I noticed the names God! Are you trying to telling me something? Are you trying to get my attention? What is it that you want me to do? Do you want me to look for this person? I am not sure I want to do that. What does she think of me? Would she be ashamed of me, or maybe angry with me? Does she hate me? God I don't want to do this!"

As those thoughts whirled around in my head about what that really meant, that I might have to meet this person, my anxieties grew.   I thought I'd already dealt with this. I just wanted to put all those anxieties to rest, to put my past back where it belonged, but where was that? Maybe it was deep in my subconscious, but it was stuffed, stuffed deep, and that is where I wanted it to stay. I didn't let the enemy tell me lies about who I am. I was standing on the truth of what God said about me (at least most of the time).

Now that I look back, I realize I was fighting with God. I kept saying I didn't want to think about and deal with my past. That is when God basically told me, "It is not always about you. She is looking for you, and you need to prepare yourself and your family. There have been times that she has been close to finding you, but I have closed the door because you were not ready. Your paths will cross. You need to prepare yourself." Then I saw a picture of a puzzle completed except for one piece, I held that one missing piece in my hand, afraid to put it in its place.

His word to me was so clear, it scared me. I thought to myself, "What did God mean that she had been close to finding me? Was she really looking for me? I am sure that her life has been complete with her adoptive family. Why would someone want to look for me? This is crazy!" Could it be that I really hadn't dealt with my past? Really, how could I tell Ashley not to run from her hurt and let God heal and restore her if I haven't done it myself? As I worked around the yard, trying to brush the whole thing off, I told myself that it was just my imagination getting away from me, but I couldn't help feeling scared. Was I reading too much into this?   What did God want me to do? I didn't know if I was ready for this. I didn't want to deal with it. *Clearly, I had been running from this for over 25 years.... talk about denial and stuffed emotions!*

I really don't want to disobey God

I told Bob about my conversation with God, and he asked me what I was going to do. What a weird question, I thought. I seriously didn't want to disobey God. But as I pondered it, I realized that I was arguing with Him.

Isn't it crazy to think that we argue with God? When we clearly know what we are to do, and don't do it, that is disobeying God plain and simple.   And that was exactly what I was doing. I talked myself out of believing that God was asking me to process my past, and open the adoptive files.   I was telling myself that all of this was my active imagination.

If God really wanted me to process my past and to seek out Tabitha, His instructions would have to be a little bit clearer. Just because the cashier pointed out three times that the flowers I picked out had real names, and that name on my mums was precisely the same name on my baby's original birth certificate, didn't mean a thing. The <u>word</u> I got from God? Well, I just put it off and tried to forget it. Again, I tried to tell myself it was my imagination.

Clearly I was in denial.

So God got clearer about what He wanted me to do.

Tabitha was not a name I had seen or heard up until that time, but after the incident in Menards, it was a name that I kept running into. Even the pharmacist assistant at the local drug store was named Tabitha. I ran into that name almost daily, and each time I was reminded that God had something for me to do. "This is crazy!" I thought. "It can't be a coincidence that this name keeps crossing my path." I knew I told God He needed to be a bit clearer, but this wasn't about me, I thought, it was about Ashley and what she was feeling and processing. *"God, are you preparing me for something?"* I then remembered the Cold Case television show that struck such deep emotions within me. *"Do you want me to deal with my emotions, or are you actually asking me to look for this person, Lord? Do you want me to pray for her, Lord?"*

As I struggled to know what God was telling me, I was also worrying about Ashley. I knew that the scars on her heart needed to be healed. The negative words that Ashley was hearing were lies from the enemy. I know because I was the most miserable person walking around with all my insecurities. I remember feeling disposable, not really worth anything, and that no one would ever want to be with me. I didn't want Ashley to feel that way about herself.

I became very co-dependent believing that I had no worth. It first started with my desire to please everyone. I believed that the only reason guys dated me was because of what I could do for them. I felt I <u>had</u> to do things for them, even when I didn't want to, so that they would stay with me. I became co-dependent, not just in my dating relationships, but in all areas of my life.

I felt I could only be someone if I was <u>with</u> someone. My life really had no meaning. I wasn't important enough just being me, I had to perform. I didn't want that for Ashley. I wanted her to know the truth about what God says about her. If she didn't have the Truth to grab on to, the enemy's lies would drag her down. I know from my own experiences. *Lord God, help me help her.*

I felt like I let God down

I couldn't help feeling that I had disobeyed God. So I called a very good friend of mine who works for a State Senator. I told her what the Lord was telling me to do and asked who I would talk to about opening adoption files. She gave me Marny's name who worked in the County Clerk's office in the county where I had given birth.

With some hesitation, I called. *It wasn't like Marny knew who I was.* I shared with her that at the age of 16 I had given birth to a baby girl and she was placed for adoption, but I wasn't sure if the files were open or not. *I knew that they weren't.* I wanted to sound sophisticated, and that I had it all together, but I was very nervous. I talked without giving Marny a chance to answer my questions. I then asked her if the girl (now a grown woman) wanted to get in touch with me what steps would she have to take.

Once I gave her a chance to speak, Marny told me that when a child is put up for adoption, the original birth certificate is destroyed. The instant I heard that, sadness washed over me. I

40

felt as if I didn't matter. I was erased completely from her life. I can't explain how much that hurt me. All this time I didn't let myself feel anything. It came as a complete surprise when tears began pouring out.

As I tried to hide the fact that I was crying, Marny gently told me that she was thankful I had gone through with the pregnancy, that it was a brave, selfless thing I had done at such a young age. "So many other girls would have taken a different approach under the circumstances," she said.

I didn't feel that what I had done was brave and selfless. In fact I felt the opposite. I felt ashamed and selfish because there were things that I wanted to do with my life. Yes, I wanted her (my baby) to have nice things, but I didn't see myself as a selfless person.

Marny took my address and told me she would send a form for me to fill out to open the adoption files. As we hung up, she said, "God bless you, and good luck." Feeling emotionally drained; I went to my bedroom and cried. I wasn't sure why I was crying, but the tears would not stop.

A few days after that phone conversation, I received a letter from the County Clerk's office. This was it, the form. I opened it and was taken aback by the simplicity of it, just a few lines to fill out; it didn't even need to be notarized, just a line for a witness to sign. Not wanting to deal with it, I tucked the form away in my Bible so that no one would find it, and told myself I would fill it out later. Besides, it wasn't about me being in denial, it was about Ashley being in denial. It was about Ashley processing her emotions not me processing mine.

The envelope

I called my mom to ask what was put on the original birth certificate. *I didn't share with her what I felt the Lord telling me to do, and she didn't ask any questions.* She didn't really have much information, but Mom told me that Dad had sealed an envelope for <u>her</u> if she ever made contact with us/me. I asked my mom for the envelope. I just wanted it because it was something from my dad, for the simple fact that my dad had touched it. Dad had passed away several years ago, and I missed him. "What had he written?" I thought to myself. Maybe it was his feelings; maybe it was a journal from that summer. I didn't know why I wanted it, but I did. Though once I received the envelope fear washed over me. What was in it? What did dad have to say? Can I open it? My dad had typed specific instructions on the front of it:

Only to be opened by my genetic granddaughter who we call Tabitha.

Who would know if I opened it? It's wasn't like Tabitha was in my life. She didn't even know this envelope existed. For some reason, I couldn't open it. I felt it would be intruding on someone else's privacy. I can't explain it, but I felt conviction even at the thought of opening it. Just like the form I had gotten from the Clerk's office, I tucked the letter away where I knew no one would find it.

My Dream

Several weeks passed after tucking away the release form into my Bible. I had also pushed it from my thoughts and tried to concentrate on how to reach out to Ashley without pushing her away. *We were like magnets when you try to put two of the same sides together, the force pushes each of them apart.*

I was disturbed one morning when I awoke from a dream. It was so clear, it felt real. So real that I was questioning where I was, as I pulled myself back to reality. I don't often wake up remembering a dream, if I dream at all, but this one I did. I was in a classroom, with a baby boy. *Odd that it was a boy, not a girl.* We were sitting at a desk with paperwork that I was to fill out. There were other people sitting at desks, and they were busy filling out their own forms. It wasn't any formal kind of paperwork; it was just a blank page where I was to explain why I was giving up my baby. I remember feeling in the dream that I wasn't sure that I wanted to give him up. *Another thing about my dream I was an adult, the age I am now.* I was trying to decide what I was going to do; I was thinking that I didn't know how my children (Ashley and Kory) would take it, what they would think. Would they be hurt, or would they welcome this baby? While everyone else in the room continued to fill out their paperwork, I was just sitting there looking down at mine. All of the sudden, I was at what seemed to be an elegant restaurant. Members of a big family party or banquet were trying to pay their bills and leave. Ashley, who was the cashier, was so overwhelmed that I jumped in to assist with the crowd. Once the last couple left, I realized that I had forgotten about the baby and started to look for him, but it was too late. Someone from the agency or the family who wanted the baby had taken him before I had filled out the form explaining why I was giving him up. I remember feeling a sense of loss, but also a sense relief.

I have often wondered how Ashley and Kory would feel if this person ever entered our lives. I love them so much! I wouldn't want them to think that I loved them any less or that they had

44

been replaced, especially Ashley. My prayer was that if this person entered our lives, we could be complete as a family. Unlike Ashley, Kory didn't know about my past. He never liked to hear about the struggles I had growing up.

Sharing my dream

I shared my dream with my care giver, a person who had come along side of me as I have gone through those rough few months of my life. I asked if she thought God was trying to tell me something. I told her that I hadn't filled out the release form yet from the Clerk's office and that I felt maybe God wanted me to fill it out and mail it in.

I almost have to laugh now because it was so obvious that God was practically beating me over the head with what He wanted me to do, yet I was still questioning.

I also shared my dream with my long-time friend, Suella. She asked me a question that shook my memory. "When you were going through with all the formalities, do you remember if you wanted to change your mind about giving your baby up?"

I then remembered the sadness I felt alone in the hospital. *I don't recall my mom or dad being there with me, except during the delivery when my mom was at my side.* I am not even sure how long I was at the hospital after her birth. I felt very alone and wanted my baby to love, to fill the emptiness I felt inside. So yes, I did want to change my mind but I also remembered being told that the adoption was already final.

Clearing the confusion in my mind

I tried to clear my mind and walk. With Bob's ipod loaded with worship music, I stepped outside and walked everyday. Praying for my family, I tried to sort out the confusion I was feeling. I felt pushed by God to quit my job, so I could pray and help Ashley. So why was I feeling the pull to dig up my past? I asked God daily what His will was, and I kept waiting for the answer. I knew that the Lord wanted to heal my family emotionally, physically, and spiritually. But how and when?

Every time my past came creeping up on me, I pushed it out, telling myself this wasn't about me, but about Ashley. I didn't want to have to tell anyone about my past. Bob, of course knew about all of it. He had to deal with all my insecurities for several years after we got married.

I tried to tell Ashley about my past. She was, I think, in the ninth grade and had an assignment to do her family tree. One day she came home upset and appalled, that one of her friends found out she had a half brother she never knew about. I remember Ashley saying, "I can't believe Ally's parents never told her, which is so wrong!"

I didn't know how to handle that. It just came out of the blue and here I was at a crossroad. Do I say something or just keep things the way they are? Not wanting Ashley to be upset with me if she found out later, I tried to tell her about her half sister. I can't even remember how I told her. The complete shock that our conversation had turned in this direction had my head spinning. As I began to tell her, Ashley stopped me in my tracks. She didn't want to know. I thought that was okay with me, because I didn't want to go there. That was the end of subject, never to be discussed again.

I liked where I had my past, behind me. That was me before, not who I am now. When I started feeling fear and shame, I would stuff it. That is when the Lord told me, "I can't use you, until I free you." *Freedom from what, I thought? I am free! I was okay before all this stuff started coming up. Life is good. I don't need to go there, Lord.*

Each time I tried to push my past back down inside, as I had always done before, God wouldn't let me. I tried to focus on the kids, Bob, working in the yard, in the house, anything to get my thoughts off this path, but it was not working. It was like each time I walked around it, God would pick it back up and put it back in my path. I couldn't shake my past, and I felt fear and shame paralyze me. It's like I saw myself on the edge of a very dark forest, with dark, thick muck all around, and I was being made to walk through it. No one knew that forest existed or even that I was there. No one knew that I was being made to enter in. I felt scared. I couldn't see what I was stepping into, or if I would encounter something that would hurt me. Every time I turned to go another direction, I found myself in front of the same dark forest. Fear was getting the best of me; fear that I would be judged by other people. Will they call me a hypocrite? Again, I told the Lord, "I don't want to do this!"

A few days later I was reading in my Bible and God gave me this verse.

Isaiah 54: 4

Do not be afraid; you will not suffer shame. Do not fear disgrace; you will not be humiliated. You will forget the shame of your youth...

My past, which I thought was dealt with and so neatly tucked away, was stirring up inside of me. "Okay, Lord," I thought, "I will fill out the papers. It's not like this person will be at my doorstep tomorrow."

I did it! I signed the papers and mailed them out September 15, 2007. There, it was done, over. I could now move on and help Ashley.

Chapter Four
Guilt

Working outside one day, Ashley came home early from work. She was angry and informed me that she had quit her job. She was exhausted, and it was obvious that she had had enough of factory work. She started dumping all kinds of information on me. I had waited for weeks for Ashley to open up to me, almost feeling guilty about the time I'd spent on myself evaluating and processing my past.

I thought I was prepared for Ashley to talk with me, but I found myself shocked by what she was saying. Actually, I think it was more her emotions than what she was saying. It had so much force; it was like a ton of bricks hitting me in the chest.

In the weeks prior, I would make her angry just by asking questions to get the conversation going. Now here we were screaming at each other outside for the whole world to hear. I was yelling back at her because I wanted her to hear what I was saying. Instead I made things worse because she thought that I wasn't <u>listening </u>to her. Ashley expressed herself for 45 minutes crying as hard as she was yelling at me. Nothing she shared with me had anything to do with what had happened in Kentucky. Only that she hated living in Indiana and the fact that she had not been able to say goodbye to all her friends in Kentucky before Bob and I had moved her back.

She had told me about things she had to endure with her boyfriend Chad when we lived in Michigan, things I didn't know. He told her things that tore down her self esteem and manipulated her in awful ways. Now thinking back there were times when Ashley would be angry with Chad and didn't want to be with him. I told her that she was being hormonal because she had a real good boyfriend, a Christian young man. So I thought.

As she continued yelling at me, I couldn't help but think to myself, *"What have I done, Lord? I thought that I could help her, and with the love of her family around her she would get through this. I have failed her, Lord."*

Having no energy left to yell, she went inside to take a nap. As I helped her into her bed, I prayed that she would be able to get some rest, and I went back outside to cry. I felt so much guilt. I wasn't there for her to defend her when she was at <u>home</u>. How could I have missed the signs? I knew she had some bitterness in her heart, and I knew that there was something that was tearing at her soul. I had no idea that the bitterness was bigger than what was normal for a teenager. By telling her that she might be overreacting and that it was hormones, I was reinforcing in her mind that the hurt and anger that she felt would not be understood. I guess that was the reason she never told me what was really going on. She really believed she couldn't do any better, and that she should feel lucky to have such a *good* boyfriend.

The guilt I was feeling had a lot to do with all the things I had endured growing up. Of all people, I should have seen the signs of sexual abuse. When the kids were young, I was very cautious about who would watch them. I never allowed them to be alone with strangers. But just because you know a family, and that they go to church, doesn't mean that they have Christ in their hearts. I felt that I was such a horrible mother. Again, how could I have missed the signs? I felt like I failed her. That is when I heard God say to me, clear as day, "You can let guilt paralyze you, and not be there for her or you can let the guilt go and be the support that she needs." *No reason to feel sorry for myself and feel guilt. I wanted to be there for Ashley.*

Romans 8:1
Therefore there is now no condemnation (blame, disapproval, criticism, guilt) for those who are in Christ Jesus. Amen!

Chapter Five
Lord, Your will be done.

I was getting restless not working and not really connecting with Ashley. I felt like I wasn't helping her. I continued interceding for my family daily. As for my past, I thought the Lord just wanted me to pray for Tabitha.

I would pray a short little prayer, that she had a nice man in her life and that her adoptive parents were there for her giving her Godly wisdom, especially her mom. That was as far as I could go with my past, not dealing with my emotions just praying the best for her now in her life. God knew her needs.

I began looking for work

I was a little leery about what type of job I wanted to apply for. I would pray before turning in each application, "*Lord, You know what we need financially. You know what I need for a job, and You know what You are calling me to do. Your will be done.*"

I knew that the Lord had a plan in all this, but I wasn't sure that I understood the plan. As I talked with Ashley, I didn't feel that

God was directing our conversation. We just talked casually, discussing where she bought her new shorts or how she wanted to get her hair done, that sort of thing.

I was certain of the Lord's direction when he told me to quit my job and be home for Ashley, but now I felt like I might have missed something. I started to feeling as if I had made a mistake, and doubted that God had a plan in all of this mess. I thought that maybe this had just been a bunch of random things that happened, and now I needed to get to work.

I was excited each time I applied for a different position, thinking to myself, "This is it, my new career!!" I got called in for interviews and even second interviews. Each time I would pray before going into the interview, and each time I would get a letter in the mail saying, basically, thanks but no thanks. I was starting to feel discouraged. I always thought of myself as a woman of God who didn't need a job title to have self worth. But with no direction and no job, those feelings of self doubt and insecurity started to creep back into my heart, things that I hadn't felt about myself for a long time. Whenever I was asked, "What is it that you do?" I felt ashamed to say, "I am not working right now."

Yeah, what is it that I do? I don't even have small children at home.

I then started to do a little administrative work at the church. Although it filled some of my time, I still felt that I wasn't contributing to the household. The self talk started to become more negative each day, to the point it was all I heard. I was judgmental and criticized everything about myself and even started to criticize others. I was becoming that bitter person again, and I hated myself for it.

All the words that I used to encourage others echo in my head. The enemy hit me with these questions, "Did you really believe all that? Does God really have plans for you? Are you really forgiven for all your sins?" Each attack from the enemy would pierce holes in what little self worth I had. It was like I was hanging on the edge of a cliff and he was kicking my hands loose to make me fall into the dark canyon. I knew how lonely that darkness could feel. "I don't want to go back there Lord," I said, "Help me."

This must be why

One night I was getting ready to go out with some old co-workers of mine when we got a phone call. It was Bob's half sister Kelli telling us that Bob's mom, Aileen, had been in a terrible accident. We met at the hospital and waited while she underwent an eight-and-a-half hours of surgery on her neck, ankles and knee. It was a miracle that she was alive, but her recovery would include three to four months in the hospital.

Bob told me he needed me to be at the hospital with his mom. He couldn't be at work knowing that she was by herself. He trusted me to take care of her.

I guess that is why I haven't gotten a job. God knew I would be needed here with Aileen.

That was my job. I would arrive between 9 or 10 a.m. every day with my Bible and laptop. Each day I would pray, read scripture, and talk to Aileen. My focus then was assisting in anything I could do to encourage Aileen as she made progress daily. That kept me busy enough to push away the negative thoughts the Enemy tried to attack me with. I had a job to do, and my job was to help Aileen.

Chapter Six

Is this Georgia?

One month after her accident, Aileen was discharged from the hospital, truly a miracle. We all agreed that she could not go home, but that she would stay with us. Once she was settled at our house, we started to get into a routine. In the evening when Bob got home from work we would go into the living room to watch television and talk. Aileen would tell Bob the daily victories she had achieved, and Bob would share how things were going for him at work.

On the evening of November 2, as we were settling in trying to decide what to watch on television, the phone rang. *I will never forget this night for the rest of my life.* Thinking the phone call was for Kory, I let him answer it. As he shrugged his shoulders, he handed the phone to me. I don't get many phone calls, so I wondered who it could be.

I said, "Hello?"

The person said, "Hello, is this Georgia?"

"Yes," I said.

The next thing she said to me made my heart jump into my mouth!

"Hi! My name is Lisa, and I am your daughter," she said through sobs.

Oh my God! I couldn't believe what I just heard! Did I hear this person right? Was this it? Is this the very person I had been afraid to meet? She found me! I had so many emotions at that moment. I was excited, yet afraid. As I was trying to process what I was feeling, I was also asking myself/God what I was supposed to do. What is the "right" way to feel? What is the "right" thing to say? Is this going to be good? I was so afraid. Even though I was conversing with her, the words weren't sinking in. *She sounded so sweet. Was it really her?* We asked each other questions, talking and crying for about 30 minutes. The whole time we talked I was wondering what to say, how to react. I wanted her to feel comfortable, but I didn't know if I felt comfortable. I had so many questions running through my head as my mouth was on auto pilot. I felt compelled to tell her why she was placed up for adoption.

I don't even know if she asked me why. With all my guilt and shame, I thought that must be the only reason she called me.

Lisa told me about her fiancé Kevin and how he was good to her. She said she had wanted to know her biological mother for years, but something always kept her from seeking. Kevin encouraged her to fill out the appropriate paperwork to get information from the court. She told me she mailed the request around the 20th of September, five days after I had filed my paperwork.

How devastating it would have been for Lisa if she had finally pushed through her fears to request information about me, only to find the files closed.   Thank God He pushed me through my fears to open those files.

As we were ending our conversation, 26 years in the making, I gave her my email address and asked her to email me. I thought through email we could possibly start a relationship, whatever kind of relationship that it would be.

What are the rules with this kind of thing?

I couldn't help feeling afraid. I wasn't sure what God had in mind, but I knew this was all Him and that He had orchestrated it. But I still had the urge to run from it! I thought this was going to be another rough road of learning. I remember telling one of the pastors I knew that I wasn't sure if something I had received from God was going to be a good thing or bad. He simply told me, without knowing what was going on in my life that all things from God were good, period.

Maybe God had a job for me, I thought. Why else would Lisa find me? It was hard for me to think that God just wanted to bless me. Questions ran through my head; questions like, What do I do? What do I say? Do I email her or do I wait for her to email me? What do I share with Lisa? Do I talk about Ashley and Kory, or do I talk about my life growing up? How am I going to tell Ashley and Kory? Will they be upset? Will she call me Mom or Georgia? Does she even want another mom?

Not long after we hung up, I got an email from her with pictures. I couldn't believe it! She looked like me, and it was amazing. I just stared at them. It was like I was looking at my own pictures when I was younger. I didn't even know where to begin with my emotions. I was thrilled, yet terrified.

Could I really have Lisa in my life now? Do I deserve to have her in my life? Does she even *want* me in her life? Yes, she made contact with me.   She was curious about me: what I looked like, what kind of person I was. And of course, she wanted to know about her heritage. *As I later found out, she referred to herself as the "tan white girl."* Would she want me in her life after she got to know me?

I learned that Lisa had all the material things she needed, but as she shared things with me, I realized she didn't have unconditional love. She had to prove herself worthy of receiving any kind of love or affection. That tugged hard at my heart.

Guilt again

Again, the deceiver whispered in my ear that I had done the wrong thing by placing her up for adoption. Guilt and shame consumed my thoughts again making me afraid to be myself in my emails. I sat at the computer for hours typing and re-typing my emails, making sure I said the right things.

Not only did I feel guilty about placing her up for adoption, but I also felt guilty that in some way Lisa may have felt left out. I kept envisioning a sweet child looking into the window of our lives and wanting to be a part of it, but was never invited. Lisa never knew me. Did the void of not knowing who her biological mother was make her feel unwanted? That thought hurt me.

I also felt guilty about enjoying our emails back and forth. I thought maybe I was betraying Ashley and Kory in some way. I wanted to share her picture with them, but didn't know how to tell them. I sent their picture to Lisa and she seemed thrilled to have a sister and brother, true siblings that looked like her.

I felt my face light up and my heart grow warm each time I got a new email from Lisa. I was totally drawn to her. I checked my email every day reading over and over all the things that she shared with me.

As I continued to care for Aileen and attempt to get along with Ashley, Lisa's emails became my refuge. I could feel a bond start to form between us, and I sensed in my heart that she wanted - needed - a mother in her life to tell her that she was loved just because she was Lisa.

Chapter Seven
Telling the Kids

In each of our conversations, Lisa asked me if I had told Ashley and Kory about her. I felt bad telling her that I hadn't. She was so excited to have a half-sister and brother. I think she thought I was ashamed of her, that I didn't want her to be a part of the family. In truth, I was afraid of what Ashley and Kory would think of <u>me</u>. The feelings of fear and rejection were so overwhelming at times. I couldn't bear to think that my children would think less of me. My goal was to get them both together and share with them, that they had a half sister that very much wanted to meet them.

Such an overwhelming task! All I wanted was for the reunion to be painless and joyful. I prayed that we would all accept each other.

I was afraid that Ashley would feel pushed aside. I also was afraid that she and Kory would become angry with me. My plan was not working. I couldn't get them both to stay home long enough to talk to them. So I told Ashley first. As we were in the kitchen, I told her that I had something to share with her. Right away she asked if I was pregnant.

"No, I am not pregnant," I said.

"You found your other daughter?" she asked.

I was shocked that she nailed it. There was no more beating around the bush. How did she know? Did she sense it? Had God prepared her for this?

I said, "No, she found me."

Ashley acted surprised and excited, but I think she had some idea that Lisa and I were in contact. As I tried to tell Ashley how the whole thing unfolded, and my struggle to find the words to tell her and Kory, she seemed preoccupied with her own thoughts. As soon as Ashley heard I had pictures of Lisa, she asked to see. *Once she saw them, I couldn't read her reaction. Ashley acted like she was excited, but I wasn't sure.*

I wasn't as nervous telling Kory about Lisa. I explained that I had been taken advantage of when I was 15 and had become pregnant. Because of the circumstances, I placed my baby up for adoption. After 26 years she has found me and would like to meet us. Kory's response was the same as Ashley's when he saw her picture. "She really looks like you mom," he said. Their first introduction was done via email. I didn't read what they said to her, but I hoped they could have dialogue before the reunion face to face.

So, when should we meet?

I really wanted to meet Lisa, but wasn't sure what I needed to do to prepare for the reunion. I knew she would have a lot of questions, but I wasn't sure I could answer them. I had stuffed my past so deep that I didn't even know if I could find my emotions, my thoughts, and my fears. We set the date for February 22, 2008. I never got to hold her, not even once, after I gave birth to her. I didn't even get to see her, not a glimpse of her hair or her little hand. She was quickly removed from me by the nurses. And to think I was actually going to meet this 26-year- old person, my daughter.

From the beginning, babies know their moms. They feed them, care for them and love them. There is a natural bond. This was different. Yes, she was my daughter, but she didn't know me. Would she accept me? Would she even like me? I had so many feelings to process before meeting Lisa. I knew God was pushing me to remember, but as the days went by, I kept putting it off. I still couldn't go there; I couldn't push myself to remember.

As Lisa and I grew more comfortable with each other through email, we started to talk on the telephone. She shared more things about her childhood and talked about her fiancé Kevin, how they had been engaged for a while as they were saving the money to pay for their wedding on their own. She also told me that she couldn't decide on a wedding date.

Because Lisa didn't understand unconditional love she had a hard time understanding Kevin's love.

In one of our conversations, she announced that she had picked her wedding date. She wanted to get married on May 11, 2008, Mother's Day, and she asked me if I could be there. I couldn't believe it! After we got off the phone, I just sat quietly and cried. My head whirled again. This was unbelievable! Lisa wanted me to be at her wedding. Then oh- my- gosh thoughts ran through my head like, her family and friends will be there, what will they think of me? Will Ashley and Kory be okay with this?

Still hiding from my past

The more God brought up my past, processing it, the more I pushed to talk with Ashley about processing hers. One day when she had enough of me pushing her into a conversation, she yelled at me, "Mom, this isn't about me, it's about you!" That statement took me by surprise, because I kept telling God that it wasn't about me, it was about Ashley. *God is this really about me processing my past?*   But again I brushed it off and began pushing harder for a job. With Aileen back at home now, I spent hours online looking for jobs, filling out applications, and going to interviews, all the while thinking in the back of my head about what I needed to do, what I was supposed to do - process the past.   God must have thought that I was the most stubborn person, but He still blessed me with a job! I was to start the very Monday after the reunion.   Then God said to me, "There! You got your job! Now stop running and give yourself time to process your past before you meet Lisa."

Reluctant as I was, I stopped everything. I stopped worrying about Ashley, Kory and Bob. I stopped thinking about the fact that I needed to get into shape. I stopped worrying about getting the house cleaned, and how the bills would get paid. I stopped being busy and allowed myself the time to process the past- to go back to when I was 15 years old.

Chapter Eight

This is what I remember

I don't remember being pregnant, other than gaining weight. I don't remember feeling the baby move or the details of the monthly doctor visits. I remember only that the adults in the waiting room would make me feel very uncomfortable. The whispering was unbearable.

I remember my great aunt and uncle came to visit from Tennessee. I was told to leave the house so that my family wouldn't have to explain my situation. It was hurtful, because my great uncle would call me his little princess and always made me feel special. I thought to myself that if he saw me in the condition that I was in I wouldn't be his princess anymore. I don't begrudge my parents or think they were bad. I know they did what they thought was right. But to me it confirmed the shame I already felt inside.

Once in a while I would go to the grocery store with mom just to get out, but I would get judgmental looks from people. Mom and I both knew that people were talking about me. The whispers, "She is too young," "What a shame," would be some of the things that we would hear. I remember acting like it didn't bother me, that I was okay. I just detached myself from my emotions, saying to myself again, *"This isn't happening to me, this is just a dream."*

I don't recall having any deep conversations with my parents. I kept a journal and wrote in it a lot, but after I had the baby someone got a hold of it and read my inner most thoughts. Feeling very exposed and crushed, I could no longer trust anyone, not even a piece of paper, with my inner emotions.

One day when everyone was gone I destroyed my journal. I went outside and I tore out each page and burned it. I felt devastated, like I was betraying myself. I wasn't just destroying pages of a journal; I was destroying a part of my life, a part of me. I even destroyed pictures that were taken of me during that summer, all from the shoulders up.

Today, I wish I hadn't burned that journal. I've blocked much of that summer out of my mind. I want to re-connect with that person, even though it was me. For years I had worked hard to erase that person from memory, and now God wanted me to bring her back.

The Hospital

I vaguely remember the trip to the hospital. I don't remember who drove, or being admitted. I do remember turning myself off during the labor. I detached myself from what was happening, and just did what I was told to do. I was crying on the inside, but would not allow myself to cry on the outside. After the delivery when I was more coherent, I heard my baby cry, and it tore me up. I wanted to hold her, but I was not allowed to. I didn't feel that the nurses had the right to be so protective of my baby. Or did they?

Because it was difficult for me to be there, I was moved to a different floor. Not sure how to feel, I cried alone by myself. I felt empty, sad, and left out in some way. If I could just get home, I thought, I could get my life back and not be in this dream. A dream that was so heavy I felt like I was going to drown, and not be able to find Georgia ever again.

Who is Georgia?

I remember asking myself, "Who am I?" How am I supposed to act? Can I go back to the Georgia that I was before all this? Before all this happened, I was just beginning to try to understand myself and who I was, what I could be.   So, in a way, I really didn't know how to find Georgia?

Once I got home, I felt disconnected from my family.   I could only assume that they were all disappointed in me.   All I felt was shame and loneliness.   On the day I came home, I remember my brothers sitting on the couch well behaved, almost as if they were sitting at attention. *This isn't like them, especially the twins who were always full of energy.* They didn't look my way as I walked up to them.   They looked straight ahead, but I could see their eyes follow me through the room.   It was like I was in the twilight zone.   I felt like I was walking into a room of people who looked like my family, but I was an outsider.   It was like a dream, and I wasn't really there.   I felt like someone hit the mute button, or better yet, the pause button, and I was the only one moving in the room. *It was really eerie; even now it gives me a lost feeling.* What do my brothers really think of me?   Are my parents angry with me, sad that I place my baby up for adoption? Can they even look at me the same way that they did?

Overwhelming shame washed over me as I made my way to my bedroom.   As I closed the door I told myself that I didn't want to ever come back out.

Back to school

I tried to put on the jeans I wore before all this happened, and to my great disappointment I couldn't get them zipped and buttoned. To this day, I can remember lying on the floor of my bedroom crying and thinking nothing would ever be the same again. I then made a conscious decision to cut the past summer totally out of my life, like cutting someone out of a photo. Just like burning my journal, I wanted to burn everything about that summer from my memory. I would put on my favorite jeans and walk back into the hallways of my high school as if those months never happened. I thought I could be that same Georgia I was before, I would find her. I would walk back into the school unnoticed, and I would just blend right back in.

So I thought...

Judgment

It wasn't long after I got back to school I found that everyone had an opinion about my baby being placed for adoption. One day, I was waiting in the lunch line and a group of girls in front of me began judging me. With great sarcasm, the leader of the group asked, "What kind of mother are you, giving up your baby for adoption? We can't believe you did such a horrible thing like that! You're the worse mom ever. You don't deserve to be a mom."

Lie number one, a lie I held onto for years: I am a bad mother.

It wasn't unusual for the guys in my class to call out awful things to me. I knew before all this happened that I wasn't much to look at, so in that respect things were the same as before.

Lie number two: I am not attractive and no one would want me.

There is always that one guy

I was okay being in the back corner of the classroom where no one would bother me. I would never share my opinions or even allow myself to join in any classroom chatter. At times it was lonely, but I felt safe there. I would not go against the flow of things, and I would never draw attention to myself. I would just die inside if I was the last one to walk into the classroom.

In class one day, the new guy that all the girls were buzzing about started to talk with me. I thought to myself, "What is he doing? He is drawing attention to me." I would give him one word answers so that I didn't have to talk to him. Why would anyone want to know my opinion on things? The other guys in the class told him that it wasn't cool to talk with me, but that didn't seem to bother him. Each day he would talk with me, drawing me out of the seclusion. Over time, I was able to look at him as we talked instead of at my hands and feet. I had the tendency to look at my feet when I talked to people, even as I walked down the halls at school.

One teacher wanted to help me, he told me that I needed to hold my head up, that I had nothing to be ashamed of. He asked me to stay after school and practice walking down the hall, holding my head up and looking straight ahead, instead of my feet. Every time I looked at my feet, I had to walk down another hall. To this day when I am looking down at my feet, I can hear him say "Hold that head up, young lady! You can't do anything until you learn how to be yourself."

Chapter Nine

Being real with my battles

I had forgotten how real the demons in my life could be, how hard they attack and how hard they were to fight off. Before I found out what it truly meant to be a child of God, I was tormented with the lies that the Enemy convinced me to believe. It was an endless; viscous cycle. I listened to lies that caused me to react to everything. Then I would feel embarrassed or ashamed, because I knew deep down inside I was wrong, which would then lead me to hate myself even more. Each time something arose in my life, I couldn't think rationally or handle it as I should have. No, I reacted in ugly ways confirming everything the Enemy was saying about me.

I was afraid of failing in every area in my life: as a wife, mom, daughter, sister and even as a friend. On the outside I appeared happy, life was good, but on the inside I was falling apart and badly beaten by internal attacks from the Enemy. I was constantly seeking approval, pushing myself harder and harder. I became driven to do more things and to do them better. In doing so, I was seeking to be loved and accepted. Conditional love: that is what I thought it was all about. "If I do this and do it better than anyone else, I will be accepted, I will be loved."

When I did things, whether it was washing dishes or landscaping the lawn, I would not accept help from others because once finished I felt I was important and valued by others. Whenever I got affirmation or compliments, I wouldn't accept them graciously because in my head I assumed that the person was lying to me.

Low self esteem led me to feel I was not good enough and that I did not bring enough into relationships, any kind of relationship. I felt I was being judged and criticized by other people. In turn, I had a chip on my shoulder. I thought if they wanted to criticize me, I would criticize them. The criticism and judging was all in my head, not actual words spoken to me, which would again make me react in ugly ways.

I didn't trust anyone. So I didn't let people too close to me, not even Bob. I felt that if I shared my fears or insecurities, I would be rejected. No one knew the battles that were going on inside of me, the harassment I constantly felt from the Enemy. Someone once told me that when my children were younger I wouldn't give them the time of day and that I would never talk to them. I know now it was because I was walking around with this negative self talk. My days were filled with an internal conversation that kept me from talking with people and making new friends. I withdrew to the point that others thought that I was a snob. I didn't think of myself better than others, I thought just the opposite.

I sought out self improvement books thinking I would gain some sort of secret to bettering myself. I was looking for ways to make myself whole and to feel normal. Because that I was always working on self improvement, it was very difficult for me, or anyone around me, to have fun. I took myself and life too seriously. *Sometimes I still do.*

Not only was I tormented during the day, the Enemy had my nights, too. I had dreams, awful, detailed dreams of Bob leaving me because I was not good enough, desirable enough. It was so real to me that I constantly questioned his commitment to me and our marriage. I believed that there was another woman in his life because I didn't think I could meet all his needs. It got to the point that I quizzed him about every detail of his day. I believed that every conversation that he had with people – women - was more stimulating and interesting than what I had to say. But I wasn't able to have a conversation with him; it was more like an interrogation. Everything Bob said to me got distorted. I only heard what was filtered through the lies I believed about myself. It got to the point that Bob was afraid to say anything to me. Choosing his words carefully, communication with me became too exhausting. As a result, he avoided me all together, which again confirmed my suspicions that he didn't want me. Bob didn't know how to handle my insecurities. When he needed some space to be with his friends, I took it as, "I don't love you and don't want to be around you." I remember him saying to me one day "I can't fix you." And he couldn't, especially when Bob really didn't know what or who was tormenting me day and night.

I was so miserable; I could not meet the unrealistic expectations I had on myself. The world I lived in was very lonely and dark. I could not take it anymore. One day sitting in the garage crying, I said this little prayer "God, if you are real, please come and help me because I can't live this way anymore. I hate myself and I cannot stand who I have become."

God's compassion on me

It is truly by the grace of God that HE placed different people in my path. Women, who have prayed with me, and spirit-lead pastors who have taught me what the Scriptures say about who I really am, a child of God. At first it was hard for me to understand that God loved me. John 3:16 – "For God so loved the world (*me*) that HE gave His only Son, that whoever believes in Him shall not perish, but have everlasting life." That God created me. Ephesians 2:10 – "For we are God's workmanship, created in Christ Jesus..."

That HE had plans for me. Jeremiah 29:11 – "For I know the plans I have for you, declares the Lord, plans to prosper you and not to harm you, plans to give you a hope and a future."

As I learned about who God is, I was able to start to trust HIS words. Each day, I would repeat those verses, and I started to grab a hold of those truths for myself. I kept reminding myself that the Creator of the entire universe created me and that I had worth in His eyes. I was then able to fight back against the Enemy's lies. As I went to bed, I prayed protection over my dreams and used my God given imagination to see His hands protecting me as I slept.

When people talked to me, I started to really listen. I pushed out the assumption that they were criticizing or judging me and really listened to what they were trying to communicate. I was letting their words filter through what God's word says about me, and as I listened I was able to respond, not react. I started to have conversations. As I looked towards the light, the darkness that I lived in began to lift, and I was able to start living the life that God intended me to live.

Chapter Ten

The Reunion

I walked through the dark forest of my past as God had asked. I relived the feelings and emotions during that summer in 1981. It was now real to me. It wasn't just a dream or a story I vaguely remembered. It all really happened to me. It was a part of who I am, and I was now ready to meet Lisa.

We agreed to meet on neutral ground, neither at her place nor mine, we made weekend reservations at the same hotel. The plan was that I would first meet Lisa alone in her room, and then after an hour or so, I would introduce her to Bob, Ashley, and Kory.

As I walked up to her room, my heart felt like it was in my throat. It was pounding so hard I was sure everyone could take my pulse just by watching the side of my neck. "I hope my makeup looks good. Is my hair okay? Do I look good in this outfit?" These were the questions that ran through my head. I must have stood there for several minutes, pushing myself to knock on the door. If I didn't do something soon the hotel employees were going to think I was up to no good. I knocked and it took a few moments for the door to open. There she was in person. Lisa... she is beautiful! It was very hard to control my tears so that my makeup wouldn't get messed up, but oh well! The hotel does have tissues. I stood there in front of Lisa taking her all in: her eyes, her hair, and her body frame, everything about her. I didn't want her to feel uncomfortable but I couldn't stop staring. She was doing the same thing, even her fiancé Kevin was looking at me. Oh my gosh! It was so uncomfortable, yet exciting.

What do you say? Really, what are you supposed to say?!

Again, my thoughts were whirling inside my head. This is her, this is really her! Oh my gosh! What am I doing? What does she think of me? To tell you the truth, I am not sure what I said, or if I even made sense. I think I told her a little about the situation back then, and that I wanted her to have all the things that I couldn't give her. She told me a little more about her search for me, and how when she saw a woman with dark hair and olive complexion, she secretly asked herself, "Is that my mom?" I left her room after about 45 minutes and returned back to my room, fixed my makeup and waited for her and Kevin to knock on our door. I then introduced Bob and Kory to Lisa. We made small talk in the room, and then proceeded to the restaurant where Ashley was waiting with her boyfriend.

I understood that Ashley needed a little more time to deal with this. It wasn't like she didn't already have enough to deal with.

Lisa's wedding

It was all moving too fast. Six months prior, I got a phone call from Lisa, and now I was at her wedding with her closest friends and family. I couldn't even talk. I was so overwhelmed with everything!

I was instructed to go to the hotel room where Lisa and the bridal party were getting ready. As I tried to gain my composure I found myself praying, "Lord, help me" over and over in my head. Again, I found myself in front of another door scared to knock. *Who is inside this room? Lisa's closest family members and friends. Oh my word! Can I do this?* I can't even explain what I felt as I walked through the door. I knew everyone was waiting to see what I looked like, or at least I thought they were, and there I was walking into the room with my comfy travel clothes on.

I made my way to Lisa as her hairdresser was doing her hair, and the photographer zooming around getting pictures. I stood before Lisa trying my best to look poised, not wanting to cry. I told her we made the trip okay and that I was going to go back to my hotel room to start getting ready. I also told her that she was beautiful and that I was so blessed that she wanted me there. I stayed long enough to meet everyone and then I tried to make a graceful exit.

As the ceremony unfolded I had to keep pinching myself because I couldn't believe I was there to witness her wedding. The wedding was beautiful, Kevin and Lisa looked beautiful. I could tell that they truly loved each other.

At the reception, the photographer was taking pictures of everyone as they settled at different tables. I wasn't sure where to sit. Ashley and Kory brought dates, so they found random spots at different tables, but I was standing by myself. Bob wasn't even next to me. In the shuffle of things, we got separated. *Do I sit with Lisa's friends and family or do I sit with Kevin's? But the problem with that was her family was sitting with his. I just wanted to run and hide.* I think my thoughts were written across my face because Lisa's aunt came up and gently invited me and Bob to join her at her table. Once at the table and safely seated next to Bob, I felt a little more comfortable. *"Bob is with me now I will be okay I thought to myself."* Everyone at the table was talking about the newlyweds, how beautiful the ceremony was, and how gorgeous Lisa looked. Then the stories started, Lisa's aunt and uncle started to share some stories of the early years of Lisa's life. As I imagined her in those stories I began losing my composure. As I fought back the tears, I nudged Bob to let me out so I could run to the ladies room. I needed to pull myself together. Lisa's aunt came to my rescue and talked with me a bit as I tried to fix my makeup. It took every ounce of strength I had to walk back to the reception. I was somewhat embarrassed that I was so emotional. Then Lisa's father-in-law came up to me and said, "We love Lisa, she is a wonderful, sweet young lady, and we accept her as one of our own. I just want you to know that you are part of the family now, too." I smiled and thanked him for the kind words, and then he continued to say, "It is amazing how much you and Lisa's mannerisms are the same, some of your facial expressions are exactly like hers." Fighting off tears yet again, I kept my composer and enjoyed watching my "three" children dance at the reception.

With all the *"firsts"* that I'd missed in Lisa's life, I felt honored that she asked me to witness the testimony of her love for Kevin, and that she wanted me to be a part of the memory that would be etched in our hearts forever.

What an awesome God we have, to give me the opportunity to be there at Lisa's wedding day is truly amazing!

September 5, 2008

In the past, around the beginning of September, I would get down, almost melancholy, and depression would wash over me. As I stepped back from the craziness of my life to ask myself why, I realized it was around the time of her birthday. I never allowed myself to go any further than that with my thoughts. I didn't want to explore my emotions. I brushed it off as just another day, and went about my daily routine. Another year would pass, and another layer of denial would be applied to my past.

But this year was different. I started planning in June what I would do for Lisa's birthday. I asked for the day off from work so that I could drive down to surprise her. Kevin, her husband, helped me by keeping Lisa's schedule cleared for me. I was actually going to spend time alone with my daughter on her birthday - the same person I was so afraid to meet; the person I could never hope to have a relationship with. I was a little afraid, but it was so obvious that God had His hand in this whole thing and I could rest in Him knowing it was going to be okay. It is hard to explain what I felt. It was Lisa's 27th birthday, and I was there. I wanted her to know that her birthday was special to me, and that the past was behind us, and I was looking forward to spending some time with her and getting to know the woman that she has become.

One on one time with Lisa! I couldn't believe it. There were times that I had to mentally pinch myself. We talked and Lisa showed me pictures of her life growing up. It was hard not to feel bad about time lost, but the joy of being with Lisa now overcame those feelings. I couldn't have asked for a better time with her talking and laughing. At times as we talked I saw myself in Lisa during my younger years, the way she would rub her nose or toss her hair. It was truly amazing.

I can't use you until I can free you

Before leaving on the birthday weekend, I shared in confidence with a co-worker, a person I thought I could trust, about Lisa. When I got back to work, to my shock, she openly called me out on it in front of another co-worker. I couldn't believe she would expose me. I seriously felt naked right in front of my other co-worker. Then I remembered other remarks that had been said to me by others, and it started to become clear to me. She must have exposed my life to others this whole time.

All the old emotions I felt in the past washed over me. Anger, shame, and guilt, the whole weight of it was so overwhelming.

I couldn't even think to do my job. All the insecurities I felt and battled in my past started to cut back into my soul.

I visualized a long dark hallway with doors. As each one opened, another would open, a domino effect, if you will. The demons were coming back, judging me, criticizing me, and accusing me. This torment went on for a few days. I shared with a friend, from our church, how I felt about what my co-worker had done to me, and she asked me why I was keeping it a secret. She also asked if I was feeling shame, or if I was afraid of people judging me. It was both.

I stood in that cold, dark hallway of open doors feeling that I had no self worth. That is when I made the decision not to go back there, to the time when I was being tormented by my demons or shame. Standing on what I know to be true of who God says I am, I pushed those negative thoughts out of my mind. In so doing I visualized myself reaching out to close that first door, and as I took that step in faith, instantly all the doors slammed shut. In that moment, God whispered in my ear, "I can not use you until I can free you."

We all have a story, a testimony of how God has shown His love to each of us. God just wants us to be honest with our pain and our struggles. I was once told that I was a very private person.

As I thought about it, I realized that I did keep a lot of things to myself. That is when God asked me, "How can I get the glory in your victories if people don't know about your struggles? He then said, "I need you to be real and sincere with your story from your heart, so that you can connect with people. Then you will be able to share your hope and faith that only comes through ME."

God wants to be active in our lives, guiding us through our struggles. He is cheering for us. He loves us, unconditionally.

I illustrated it this way to Bob. When we cheered for Ashley as she ran cross country, we were not cheering because she was in the top two runners. We were cheering because she was just doing it, running. God is cheering us on to just do it, to run in faith, taking one step at a time.

Finally

I didn't even realize that I was scared of my past, for years I kept everything buried and suppressed. I was hiding from something. I was hiding from myself. I didn't want to experience the vulnerability I felt when I was younger. I was scared of it all. I didn't want to acknowledge that person, even though that person was me. But God wanted to heal me, to free me of my past. Over the years, I let Him have different areas of my heart, but not my whole heart.

Let me describe it like this:

Take a piece of clay and roll it in a ball. Put a big hole in the center and then close the bottom of the ball. The clay looks round and solid, but there is still a hole in the center. Now take this clay ball and make marks on it, scratches and divots from being bumped around. Each day cover the ball with another layer of clay and put more scratches and divots in it. Now repeat this last step for years. What happened to the hole? It got deeper and deeper in the center. That was my heart. Over the years, I showed God those scratches and divots, and HE has smoothed them out, healing the marks on each layer that were engraved on my heart.

But I would not admit that there was a hole in the center. Even though God knew about the hole, He waited patiently for me to trust Him enough to show him my deepest wound of all.

I finally came out of hiding, and have trusted Him enough to show Him the hole; to show HIM the little girl crying in the corner of my life.

I visualized God picking that little girl (me) up out of the corner. HE listened as I told Him everything that had happened. With tears in His eyes, He said gently and lovingly, "It is all covered by the blood of My Son, Jesus."

So how is it I can help Ashley?

As I prayed and cried to God asking how I could help Ashley, He told me that I couldn't, but HE could. I know Ashley's wounds go deep into the core of her soul, but I also know that God can restore, heal and set her soul free. I stand on my faith and continue to pray that Ashley would trust God enough to let Him begin to heal the scratches and divots of her heart. I also pray that God will bring women into her life to show her the truth about who she is in Christ Jesus. I know that as Ashley learns to trust God and overcomes her fear, the past, she will one day show Him the deepest wound of all, the hole that is in her heart. That is when God will set her free. "Thank You, Jesus!"

Just a note

It was very hard for me to visit the past and re-live it. God wanted to free me from my past. He didn't want to hurt me by re-living it. He wanted to heal me. Yes, it was very painful, and I have experienced many attacks emotionally. I know the Enemy wanted to keep me in this bondage. I have cried more these past months over this part of my life than I ever had before. It is over, I know that the Enemy is defeated and can no longer hold my past over me. It is all covered by the blood of Jesus!

God said to me, "I can't use you until I can free you."
I am now free. Amen.